Book of Centuries

Belonging to:

_____

Begun:

_____

© Copyright 2014. Kathy Weitz
Cottage Press
www.cottagepress.net
Cover Design by Jayme Metzgar

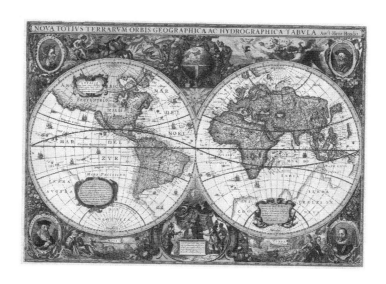

...for in history you have a record of the infinite variety of human experience plainly set out for all to see; and in that record you can find for yourself and your country both examples and warnings; fine things to take as models, base things, rotten things, through and through, to avoid.

~Livy, *Early History of Rome*

In the

Adam was notawake when he took his ribe he was in a deep sleep.

God made Adam feel alone before making Eve.

- Day 1: God created light and seperated it from darkness.
- Day 2: God created sky between the upper water and the lower water and called it heaven
- Day 3: God made hills and feilds sprout from the seas.
- Next: God created grass, bushes, seeds, and trees with fruit.
- Day 4: God created the son, and the moon, the stars, and the seasons,
- Day 5: God created the birds and the fish.
- Day 6: God brought forth living creature and then made mankind in his image.

When Satan took the form of a snake he had wings.
Adam decided to eat the fruit that god forbid for Eve.

- Satan took the form of a snake and decieved Eve. she didn't wan't to be alone and told adam to eat it with her. And they knew good and evil. They felt horrible stopped doing their chores and hid from god.

They realized they were naked and hid from god.
God put a guard with four heads to gaurd the garden.
They were given hope for the future

- Adam and Eve were cursed and banish from the Garten. But were told that a son of god will crush satan.

beginning . . .

Men began

When Cain was born Adam and Eve thought he would defeat Satan.

when Cain left he went with his wife.

Down Cains line TublaCain was an inventor Metallurgist.

Somewhere in seths family tree the promised seed would be born.

● Adam and Eve had sons and daughters and taught them to sacrifice and live for god. Later Cain became jelous of abel and Killed him. And Cain was cursed.

● Cain wandered for his whole life his Kids settled down. he started a city and left it with his son Enoch and the citie's people moved away from God.

● After Cain left Eden Adam and Eve had a son named Seth and made sure to teach him of God. One day God removed the cheribum, the litning bolt, and the tree of Knowing good and evil. Adam and Seth taught about god. And they found out that the earth will soon be flooded by water so they built monuments that would tell the survivors of God.

to multiply . . .

A flood

of water . . .

5000 B.C.

2500 B.C.

2500 B.C.

2200 B.C.

2IOO B.C.

2100 B.C.

2000 B.C.

1900 B.C.

1900 B.C.

1800 B.C.

1800 B.C.

1700 B.C.

1700 B.C.

1600 B.C.

1600 B.C.

1500 B.C.

1400 B.C.

1300 B.C.

1200 B.C.

1100 B.C.

1000 B.C.

900 B.C.

800 B.C.

800 B.C.

700 B.C.

600 B.C.

500 B.C.

400 B.C.

400 B.C.

300 B.C.

200 B.C.

200 B.C.

100 B.C.

In the fullness

of time . . .

A.D. I

A.D. 100

A.D. 2OO

A.D. 200

A.D. 300

A.D. 400

A.D. 400

A.D. 500

A.D. 600

A.D. 800

A.D. 800

A.D. 900

A.D. 1000

A.D. 1100

A.D. 1300

A.D. **1400**

A.D. 1400

A.D. 1500

A.D. **1550**

A.D. 1550

A.D. 1600

A.D. 1650

A.D. 1700

A.D. 1700

A.D. 1750

A.D. 1800

A.D. 1820

A.D. 1860

A.D. 1880

A.D. 1900

A.D. 1910

A.D. 1920

A.D. 1950

A.D. 1960

A.D. 1970

A.D. 1980

A.D. 1990

A.D. 2000

A.D. 2000

A.D. 2010

A.D. 2020

A.D. 2020

Maps & Notes

Maps & Notes

Maps & Notes

Maps & Notes

Maps & Notes

Maps & Notes

Maps & Notes

Maps & Notes

Maps & Notes

Maps & Notes

Maps & Notes

Maps & Notes

Maps & Notes

Maps & Notes

Maps & Notes

Maps & Notes

Maps & Notes

Maps & Notes

Maps & Notes

Maps & Notes

Maps & Notes

Also available from Cottage Press

Classical Language Arts Curricula

Language Lessons *for* Children
Primer One & Primer Two

Charlotte Mason style gentle lessons in grammar and composition for early elementary students—the perfect preparation for more rigorous language arts in later years. Features copywork and narration lessons drawn from classic children's literature and poetry. Includes nature and picture study lessons each week.

Coming Soon

Language Arts *for* Grammar Students
Language Arts *for* Intermediate Students

Grammar and composition lessons structured around the fable and narrative stages of the progymnasmata. Includes strong sentence diagramming component along with basic studies in poetry, literary terms, figures of speech, and figures of description.

In Production

Poetics & Progym *for* Upper School I
Poetics & Progym *for* Upper School II

Essay composition and beginning rhetoric structured around the classical oration and the classical progymnasmata. Includes in-depth study of grammar, sentence diagramming, poetry, literary terms, figures of speech, and figures of description.

. . . and much more to come! Visit cottagepress.net to see our complete offerings.

51027550R00085

Made in the USA
Lexington, KY
09 April 2016